LEADERSHIP

How to make difficult co-workers respect,
admire and follow you

Disclaimer

The information in this book is presented for purposes of education and information only. The author is in no way liable for any outcomes sustained by the reader as the direct or indirect result of the implementation of any advice contained herein. If you know or suspect that you require professional help you must consult with a suitably-qualified person.

CONTENTS

YOU ARE A LEADER!

Who is this book for?

Congratulations! If you've picked up this book, you have probably earned a leadership or management role. This may represent a promotion for you, and a new challenge that will stretch you professionally and personally. You may be lying awake at night, anxious about what awaits you. You might be wondering whether your colleagues will respect you, whether your team will look up to you as an authority figure, whether others in the workplace will perceive you differently as a result of your new role, whether you can deliver on targets for your line manager...and the list goes on. You have a lot to think about, and you may be starting to panic.

Fear not. This book can help. We're going to look at the most common fears and issues new leaders face, and why it's important to take a pro-active approach to developing your own leadership potential.

Even the most accomplished leaders started where you are now – nervous about this next stage in their professional lives. The way you are feeling now is completely normal, and can be overcome as long as you are willing to put in the time and effort to understand the most common leadership obstacles new leaders face and how they can be solved. You will learn how to win over even awkward colleagues!

Let's start by taking a closer look at some those worries.

1. That you won't be competent; that your knowledge simply won't be sufficient for the role.
No matter how long you have been with a company, you may still feel as though you lack the relevant training for your new role. If you are moving to a new organization to take up a management role for the first time, then you also face the usual anxiety that comes with being a 'new hire.'

2. That people who have showed faith in you will be disappointed.
Being awarded a promotion by a long-term mentor or manager you respect is a terrific compliment, as is earning a glowing reference from a former employer that allows you to move onto a better-paying job with more responsibilities. However, the downside is that you may feel a sense of pressure. What if you underperform and disappoint those who have shown belief in you?

3. That you may lose some friends at work as a result of your promotion.
If you have worked with the same group of people for months or even years, there can be shifts in the interpersonal dynamics should you be promoted. You may now find yourself having to manage people you consider to be friends. This may profoundly affect your social life. You should be prepared for the possibility that if you are remaining with the same company to take up a management position, some people may not be able to perceive you in the same way, and some may

even be too envious or intimidated to continue your friendship.

4. That you will spend too much time managing people and not enough time driving the business forward.
A leader is supposed to lead, and managers are supposed to manage. However, it is possible to become too embroiled in petty details at the expense of advancing the company objectives. New managers often worry that they will spend too long in meetings, for example, at the expense of their other duties.

5. That you won't be able to handle difficult co-workers.
This may be the most worrying item on the list! There's a good reason why competent leaders are so well-respected and often well-paid: managing a team and getting the best possible performance from them is hard work for many reasons. At some point in your career as a leader – perhaps even from the first day – you will have to deal with co-workers who are ill-tempered, bossy, awkward, or just plain difficult.

It's quite a list, isn't it? Luckily, this book will tell you how to handle common problems you can expect to face. Implement the ideas you find in here and you can look forward to the following outcomes:

1. Your social skills will develop.
Once you understand what people look for in a leader and try and relate to them accordingly, you will become more comfortable in social situations. This will boost your confidence in your ability to communicate with other people and understand each of your team member's wants, needs and problems.

2. You will be able to extract the best possible performance from your team.

A good leader boosts team morale. Even when things are going badly or the company is facing multiple setbacks, an inspiring leader gets results.

3. You will be able to share your expertise with others.

An accomplished leader brings not only people skills but background knowledge to the role. As you establish yourself as a leader worthy of respect, you will be given many opportunities to impart your industry and practical knowledge to the people you manage and this can be very rewarding. Once you have been successfully leading a team for a while, you'll also be able to share another kind of knowledge – the kind that comes with fruitful management experience. You may have the privilege of mentoring other leaders, and develop rewarding professional relationships.

4. You will be able to have more influence on the company.

Promotion to a management role indicates that you have demonstrated your potential to make a lasting difference to the organization. Multiple stakeholders will be watching you to see what kind of impression you make on the company. Whilst this is nerve-wracking, it's important that you appreciate the opportunity you have been given. Prove yourself as a competent leader and your views will be respected more than ever before. This means that, increasingly, you will be able to influence the organization's direction and profits. In turn, of course, this means that you are more likely to gain further promotion and a higher salary!

Turn the page and learn how to take the first step towards being a great leader: making a positive impression on others.

7 WAYS TO WIN WITH PEOPLE

If you are to be a successful manager, you need to learn to make a great positive impression not only on your team, but also customers, your managers, and everyone else with an interest in the success of your organization.

All of the points listed in this chapter are relevant from your very first day in the role. In fact, they may even be relevant before this point, especially if you have the opportunity to meet your new team before your contract formally begins! Hopefully, your new employer will want you to feel as comfortable as possible in your new role. You may be asked to attend a 'meet the team' meeting, or even a series of meetings, in advance of your arrival. If you are offered this chance, take it! It's vital that you meet everyone on your team as soon as possible, and take the opportunity to create a positive first impression.

Creating an excellent first impression and winning people over cannot be reduced to a set of behaviors. It's more about your mindset and how you approach the situation. Think of the following guidelines as a set of principles to follow, not a set recipe for success!

Principle 1: Uphold a set of suitable values.

Think about the kind of leader that you want to be. If you take a moment to review your experience as a team member working under the direction of a more senior member of staff, you will realize that some of your managers will have much more competent and inspirational than others. In all likelihood, the sorts of leaders you have most admired in the past will have been not only competent and knowledgeable in their fields, but people of principle and integrity.

Specifically, you should be looking to model the following values: honesty, transparency, a strong work ethic, focus, compassion, commitment to the organization you serve, and the ability to be open to new ideas. Of course, your company will have their own specific set of values and core ideas, and you should look to uphold these too.

What might this look like in practice? An honest and transparent leader will share all relevant information and news with their team, whether it be positive and uplifting or not. They will never show favoritism, and they will be clear and honest about the ways in which they delegate work, assign projects and promote people. Whilst you don't have to be a workaholic to be a great leader, you should make your presence felt in the office. In short, respected leaders take care not to appear hypocritical. If you expect your team to uphold values of transparency, for example, you cannot afford to be anything less than scrupulous when making expenses claims. Act in an ethical manner and this will show through in your demeanor. In addition, it's less stressful to do the right thing in the first place than it is to try and get away with bad behavior – you will get found out one day!

Principle 2: Understand the importance of non-verbal communication. Learn to read body language and employ it to positive effect.

From the moment your team members first meet you, they will be forming judgments about you. This is natural – as humans, we judge one another all the time. However, in this particular situation the stakes for you are high, because it is hard to change peoples' first impressions and it is difficult to manage a team who don't trust you. As their leader, you want them to judge you favorably. Fortunately, you can use your body language to communicate that you are worthy of their confidence and respect.

Even if you feel nervous, make an effort to stand up straight. Imagine that there is an invisible cord running vertically from the top of your head to the ceiling and that it is pulling your head upwards so that you appear relaxed yet confident. Drop your shoulders and minimize unnecessary hand movements, as this will make you appear nervous. Make it your goal that the first time every member of your team sees you for the first time that you are smile. Don't grin like an idiot, but make an effort to relax the muscles around your mouth and jaw as you greet everyone, shaking their hands firmly but briefly. Avoid adopting submissive or defensive body language such as crossing or folding your limbs, or looking down at the floor. You have been appointed to lead, so act like it!

Principle 3: Take a sincere interest in your team members as individual people, not just employees.

The issue of whether employees should be friends with their managers is never going to die – some people believe that the best teams are on friendly terms with one another, whereas at the other end of the spectrum, others believe that managers should maintain a lot of emotional distance from those they supervise. However, it isn't controversial to say that most people appreciate being seen as individuals who have meaningful lives outside of the workplace. You won't be supervising many people who enjoy being seen as organizational drones!

Therefore, it is a good idea to make a point of paying attention to any information your team members share about themselves from the beginning. Also be sure to pay attention to any obvious visual cues – does anyone have a photo of their young children on their desk? They probably wouldn't mind if you asked after their family every now and again. Is there anyone who regularly brings in books or baked goods into the office for everyone else to enjoy in the break room? These sorts of people usually respond positively to a few questions about their hobbies and interests. Even if you couldn't care less about angel food cake recipes, it's part of your job as a leader to demonstrate that you acknowledge that everyone has a life outside of work.

Principle 4: Show that you are human too.
Remote, aloof leaders who act in such a way that suggests they are somehow 'above' everyone else are not popular. Can leading in a 'transactional' way – in which you are concerned with outcomes rather than values and teambuilding – work? Of course. However, those who aim for a 'transformational' leadership approach are more likely to develop an atmosphere of cooperation, joy and progress at work. It sounds much more relaxing, doesn't it?

Of course you need to maintain an appropriate level of professionalism at work. However, never allowing yourself to have a slightly grumpy morning or laugh at a joke told by a colleague will not endear you to anyone. Again, it can be helpful to think about the leaders you most admire. In all probability, you most admire those who are focused on their work but at the same time are unafraid to break loose once in a while.

Principle 5: Show sincere appreciation and praise.
Whether they show it or not, everyone likes to be appreciated for the work that they do. This is true even if the person in question doesn't enjoy their job, or would rather be working in a different field altogether. It doesn't matter – we all have a basic need to be needed and wanted.

Take advantage of this simple piece of psychology by giving out praise whenever it is deserved. Of course, you should never praise people just for the sake of it, as this will only earn you a reputation as insincere or desperate to win the affection of your team. Instead, aim simply to vocalize every positive thought you have about your team's performance or efforts. It's surprisingly easy to let people go unacknowledged. A simple 'Great job!' or 'Nicely done' delivered with a quick smile can make someone's afternoon.

Giving praise also conveys to others that you are essentially a positive person who likes to see the best in every situation, and this is a very attractive quality in a leader. Employees like to be lead by someone who can be relied upon to see the best in every situation. If your team doesn't already have an incentive structure in place, why not implement one? This can be as simple as an 'Employee Of The Month' certificate or a more elaborate program consisting of financial or material incentives for great performance.

Principle 6: Show that you can be flexible.
It can be tempting, especially if you are new to an organization, to dive straight in and try to implement your

ideas. This is a mistake. Remember that even when you have been hired to make a drastic difference to an existing team, you are going to be working with people who have done things in a certain way for a while, perhaps even years! Therefore, it is important to introduce changes in a sensitive way. This sets a precedent, establishing yourself as a leader who has high standards but avoids expecting miracles.

In practice, this means upholding the previously mentioned values of honesty and transparency. Everyone will be expecting you to make changes, but it is important that you explain your reasoning and processes via the appropriate channels. During times of intense change, hold weekly staff meetings in which you outline both what you are doing and why you're doing it. This is preferable to simply writing and sending emails, because in person you have the benefit of monitoring everyone's body language. This is valuable, because although it is easy to say 'Yes' or 'Great idea, boss!' in writing, it is harder to fake genuine enthusiasm in person. Therefore, holding meetings will help you better gauge everyone's reactions to your suggestions.

Another aspect of remaining flexible is to be open and receptive to feedback from those you lead. This is a significant topic in its own right, so we'll be returning to the subject at several points later in the book. For now, it's enough to say that people value leaders who can admit when they are wrong and look to others for guidance and support.

Principle 7: Keep your team challenged but not overstretched.

Along with feeling needed, human beings crave stimulation. This will vary from person to person – some seem to have a higher boredom threshold than others – but as a rule, if you want a happy team then you need to assign them sufficient work that they are engaged, but not so much that they become burned out.

This may be the hardest of the principles to implement, because it requires you to become familiar with the limitations and special talents of each team member. You can gain a head start here by asking your new employer for files or notes on each employee. If you are given the opportunity to hold a 'meet the team' meeting prior to your contract beginning, use it as your first chance to understand where their strengths and weaknesses lie. Who is the strongest communicator in the team? Who appears to be the best organized? Who works best under pressure?

Within the first few weeks, you will quickly come to appreciate how your team is currently managing their workload. It may be beneficial to ask each person to note down, for a few days, how they spend their time. If they feel overstretched, you can use this information to prioritize their tasks and work with them to establish a more realistic schedule.

On the other hand, you may find that you have among your team those whose talents are not utilized properly. Such people may perform adequately, but appear under stimulated. This is where you must exercise your responsibility as a manager to balance your subordinates' workload. In such a case, you should consider challenging them by asking them to assume responsibility for a new project or to help an overstretched co-worker.

Improving Emotional Intelligence can make a huge difference in your confidence and charisma.

THE MOST COMMON LEADERSHIP COMMUNICATION OBSTACLES

Strong communication skills are vital to successful leadership. Unfortunately, there are certain pitfalls that can cause problems for both experienced and new managers. This chapter will take you through the most common obstacles of which leaders must be aware if they are to communicate their messages and instructions to people they lead.

Overuse of business jargon.

Always aim to be clear and direct when talking to others. Do not be tempted to use corporate buzzwords or phrases if they are unnecessary. If you have to use a specific term that might be unfamiliar to the average person on the street, make sure you define it clearly at the outset and then return to plain English as soon as possible.

Using business jargon does not impress people – at least, not the kind of people you ought to care about impressing. Instead, it makes you appear unnecessarily aloof and can even create the impression that you are 'hiding' behind long words rather than addressing the issues directly. This does not inspire confidence in you as a leader.

Lack of confidence and certainty.

You must communicate confidently if you want your team to take you seriously. If you aren't sure of your own objectives, others will pick up on this and lose trust in you. Before attending a meeting or writing an email, ask yourself what it is that you are trying to convey in your message. Don't be afraid to state exactly what the purpose of your communication is – e.g., 'I've called this meeting about our new supplier this morning, because I'm concerned that the time required to manage their requirements may cost us valuable resources that are allocated to other projects.' If this sounds obvious, do it anyway. It's always better to risk over-simplification than leave people wondering what on earth you are saying, or even worse, why you are bothering to talk about it at all.

Insensitivity to cultural differences.

We live in an increasingly globalized world, and diversity in the workplace is rightly celebrated and encouraged. This can, however, present certain problems for leaders. To give a simple example, consider traditional cultural differences between western and Asian countries. In the former group of societies, a direct and individual-centered leadership style has been traditionally favored. However, in other cultures, it is considered rude to question your 'superiors' or elders, which may mean that team members from other cultures may be hesitant to offer you anything remotely resembling criticism or negative feedback. Tension may also arise if you and a co-worker are from very different social classes, or if there is a wide age gap.

There is no need to be pessimistic about differences, as in reality many people communicate well despite coming from dissimilar backgrounds. However, it is important to be aware that miscommunication can and does occur because of these issues. The solution is to keep your expectations clear regarding 'how we do things around here,' and keep these expectations for everyone. Don't draw attention to cultural differences, but aim to keep your language as accessible to as many groups of people as possible. For example, avoid in-jokes or particular cultural references that some team members may not pick up on. If you find yourself working regularly with people whose culture is alien to you, consider seeking advice from HR as to how you can avoid potentially awkward miscommunications.

Picking the wrong medium for your message.
Routine updates can be given via email, but significant information ought to be delivered in person or over the phone and then acknowledged with a follow-up email. Following an important in-person conversation, send the other party a message containing the key points raised. End the email by stating that if the other person has no objections, you assume that the email represents a valid record of the conversation. Make sure that you obtain a 'Read' receipt for the message, and keep a printed copy if the matter is especially sensitive. This can prevent disputes later.

Jumping to conclusions based on single incidents or isolated pieces of body language.
Have you ever noticed someone yawn whilst you were talking, and felt annoyed as a result? It's easy to notice a single element of someone's body language and draw negative inferences. You must resist the urge to do this, as it can result in you feeling unnecessarily anxious or angry towards your

team. Remember that yes, someone could be yawning in a meeting because they are bored, but they could also be tired or coming down with a cold. Pay attention to their broader pattern of behaviors instead. If a co-worker is generally respectful and hardworking, don't waste time becoming annoyed because they looked tired or slightly withdrawn one afternoon.

The 'Chinese Whispers' phenomenon.

If you have some vital news to impart, make sure that you are giving the information directly to everyone concerned. Do not trust that others can be trusted to pass it on with absolute accuracy! Whilst it is important to trust those directly below you in the chain of command, take the time to communicate important news and information personally. This should be done in person and then backed up by an email trail. Otherwise, you run the risk of others misinterpreting what you say, and confusion may result. In the early days of your management role, as you are still gauging the reliability and personalities of your team members, remember that the more direct you can be, the better.

Assuming that 'no questions' means 'everyone has understood.'

Have you ever been in a meeting, listened closely to what the leader was saying, yet still felt clueless when you left? Perhaps you were too embarrassed to admit that you needed further clarification, and didn't raise your hand or voice to ask questions.

It's important that you as a leader remember that just because people don't ask you any questions in a meeting, it doesn't mean that everyone has understood you perfectly. Some people might be convinced that they are the only one in the room who doesn't understand and be hesitant to ask you to explain a concept for a second or third time. The fear of looking stupid or incompetent is strong in most people.

Ideally, you will have created a supportive, positive environment in which people feel able to admit that they don't know everything, but this will take time to build that trust. In the meantime, make sure that everyone has ample opportunity to provide you with feedback or ask questions. This means allowing plenty of time at the end of meetings for questions, but it also means replying to emails promptly from the beginning of your time as a leader (so that people feel as though they can email you with questions), being regularly seen around the office (so that people can approach you in person), and always treating people with respect (so they never have to fear being mocked for asking questions).

Failing to make your presence felt.
No-one likes to be around an unreasonable, overly-grumpy or demanding leader. This is where the stereotype of the employees who cheer every time they hear that their boss will be out of the office. However, if you attempt to implement the leadership advice contained within this book, this won't apply to you! Instead, your team will actually appreciate the opportunity to see you on a regular basis.

Even if you have a private office, park in a different area of the car park to everyone else, and have a PA who guards your diary, make the effort to be accessible. Call into everyone's office as often as your schedule reasonably allows. Give your team plenty of opportunity to tell you, in person, how their work is going. Just because we now live in an age of digital communication doesn't mean that people have lost their deep-seated appreciation for in-person contact. Furthermore, demonstrating that you are willing to make the effort to see everyone proves that you value everyone's time and contribution. It will also allow you to spot problems as they arise, which can ultimately save a lot of time and agony down the road.

HOW TO SAY WHAT YOU MEAN AND STILL HAVE PEOPLE ADMIRE YOU

There's no getting away from it – sometimes as a leader you will have to say things that aren't going to be well-received. You may have to announce budget cuts, pay freezes, or break the news that a particular project will require everyone to put in some hours over the weekend. On other occasions, you will have to voice your disagreement with other peoples' opinions. From time to time, you may even find yourself in direct conflict with others. Remember that this is normal – in fact, an organization in which everyone gets along perfectly well all the time is to be viewed with suspicion, because this either indicates a culture of fear in which no-one dare voice their opinions, or a culture of conformity in which people are hired on the basis that they will fit in and cause minimum disturbance. Neither of these scenarios give an organization room to grow and innovate. To some degree, you should welcome an occasional argument or heated discussion!

Here's some more good news - there are techniques you can use to deliver difficult messages in a no-nonsense but humane manner that mean people will admire you even when you are saying things they don't want to hear. If you are still hesitant when it comes to saying what you really mean, remember that people find it hard to respect those who shy away from challenging issues. Even if it is tough to stand up for your own beliefs and opinions, living with integrity will yield you the most respect in the long run, both from others and from yourself.

Lay the groundwork by upholding the right values.
We've already addressed how important it is to maintain your integrity and transparency as a leader. Do this and you will already have prepared other people for those times when you need to deliver bad news or disagree with them. Why? Because if you have already gained a reputation for being open and honest, people won't be too surprised when you say exactly what you think and mean.

Explain your entire thought process when putting forward your point of view.
Don't leave anyone feeling confused. If you need to tell your team about a recent decision you have had to make, an opinion you hold that goes against the majority, or a significant change in policy or procedure, be sure to take it slow and start from the beginning. Simply summarizing what you believe is not enough – to convince people that you are worthy of being listened to or that your decision-making skills are sound, it is vital that you provide insight into your thought processes.

For instance, explain how and why you came to end a major contract with a certain supplier rather than just calling everyone into a room and announcing that the organization will no longer be working with them. When you take the time and effort to explain the reasons behind your actions, people will respect and trust you. They will perceive that you regard them as intelligent people who need and appreciate insight into company decisions. Taking this approach also prevents toxic, timewasting office gossip and reduces feelings of panic in more insecure team members.

Use the Sandwich Technique.

If you find yourself in a position whereby you feel as though you must disagree with a co-worker's suggestion or launch an objection, try the sandwich technique. Essentially, begin by offering a brief positive comment, followed by your main point, finishing off with another positive remark. For example, you may say something like this: .I think you've shown a lot of thought there into how you've planned out our strategy for the next quarter. But I'd like to suggest that we need to make re-organizing our logistics department our main priority here, and I don't see that well-represented in these plans. I really am impressed by the detail here, though.. This strategy makes it less likely that you will irritate other people, and shows respect for their beliefs and efforts.

Give people the respect of breaking bad news in person.

This tip shouldn't require much by way of explanation. If you need to reduce someone's hours, subject them to disciplinary action or let them go from the company, always do so in person and in a private room if possible. Even if you are releasing someone from the company, they may still tell those left behind if you were insensitive in doing so, and this may harm your reputation. Put yourself in their position and treat them as you would want to be treated.

Remain positive even in the face of bad news. Reframe it as an opportunity to do something different, new, or better.

There may be instances in your management career when you have to break terrible news to your team, for instance in the event of company closure or the passing of a co-worker. In such cases, attempting to put a positive spin on the news would be crass and insensitive.

However, much of the time, there is usually some kind of upside to be found if you look hard enough. This is a valuable skill to learn, because people like and respect leaders who acknowledge bad news yet also encourage their team to regard it as a learning experience. Before calling a meeting or sending out a message detailing negative news, try to find at least one somewhat positive outcome. For instance, although your team may have lost a contract, this may free up their time to make another project especially good.

Resist the temptation to overshare.
There's nothing wrong with a leader who feels passionate about their work and reacts to major events with strong feelings. However, it is important that you do not share absolutely everything that you think and feel. As a general rule, tell people what they need to know and what you would like to know were you in their position, but no more than that. Under no circumstance should you disclose any confidential information that those above you would rather not become common knowledge. No matter how much you trust and like your team, you can bet that somehow, you will be identified as the source of the information leak.

Practice the tough stuff out loud, alone, to perfect your tone and body language.
Public speaking is hard work for most people, and if you need to address a crowd it can be absolutely nerve-wracking, particularly if you need to impart bad news. If you haven't

engaged in much public speaking prior to your first leadership role, now might be a good point to seek out training or classes to help you develop this skill. Do this early on, before you run into your first crisis – and it's inevitable that you will, as life is unpredictable – and you'll feel better-equipped to handle the tough times ahead.

If you have to make a presentation or give a talk in which you will be required to deliver bad news, practice first. Lock the door, stand in front of a full-length mirror, and look at your body language. Check that your posture is straight, that your hands aren't twisting together or pulling at your clothing, and that you are looking straight ahead. Practice addressing the back of the room and projecting your voice by speaking from your diaphragm rather than the back of your throat. Attending a group such as Toastmaster's International can help you to perfect your technique, as can any public speaking or media training offered by your employer. You never know until you ask, so if you frequently find yourself becoming nervous when talking to groups, why not ask your manager if there are opportunities available to help you improve in this area? It isn't a sign of weakness to say that you need help. On the contrary, it shows that you are willing to take an honest inventory of your strengths and weaknesses, which makes you a desirable employee and leader.

WHAT IF PEOPLE
DISAGREE WITH YOU?

At some point - in all probability, it will come sooner rather than later – you are going to come up against people who disagree with you. This is something you need to get used to, especially if you work with a large or diverse team of people. Knowing how to handle negative feedback and differences of opinion is an essential skill for any leader.

Realize that they might be right, so hear them out.
When someone disagrees with you, is your default assumption that you must be in the right and they in the wrong? If so, you need to adjust your attitude right now. You cannot expect to be right on every occasion – no-one is perfect or superhuman. In other words, when someone pushes back against you, you ought to assume that they may have a point. They may not necessarily be completely correct in their assessment, but be prepared to concede that you should listen to what they have to say. This is particularly true if you are new to the role or to an organization. Do not dismiss someone else's opinions simply because they are less experienced, more junior, or younger than you.

If you find yourself agreeing with what they are saying, don't be afraid to acknowledge this openly.

Even if their view is nonsense, think of your reputation before you overreact.
All well and good, you may think, but what if the other person in question really is wrong, or is known to spout a lot of nonsense? You should listen to them anyway, and take them seriously. Why? Quite simply, you don't want a reputation as someone who casts aside the views of those they lead. You want a reputation as a leader who is willing to stand firm in their beliefs but who also welcomes points of view that differ from their own.

Therefore, it is important that you grant the person who is disagreeing with you sufficient time to air their grievance. Handle this in the most discreet and professional manner possible. For example, it is always better to conduct sensitive discussions behind closed doors rather than conduct a shouting match in the middle of an open-plan office. Setting up a meeting with a formal beginning and end time also allows both of you to prepare what you will say in advance, which ensures that everyone gets the opportunity to feel heard.

See disagreements as a sign of success.
Don't be surprised or upset when people push back against your ideas – it's a sign of a positive workplace when people can respectfully disagree with their line manager. It doesn't mean you have failed. It just means you have final responsibility to take into account all the available information and come to a sensible, well-informed decision. Employees who can challenge their managers can even save lives in some situations. They should feel able to point out impending

catastrophes and suggest better, safer ways of conducting organizational activities. So make you stay open to what others say, and don't let your pride get in the way.

Your own manager, if they understand what it truly means to be a great leader, ought to be impressed that you expect your team members to disagree with you from time to time. They will feel reassured that you aren't dangerously arrogant

Get a record of the conversation, and ask for witness statements if applicable.

In most cases, disagreements are low-level and can be sorted out with a few minutes of constructive conversation. However, you may occasionally be drawn into a more heated argument with a coworker. If this is the case, you need to focus on three things:

1. Remaining calm;
2. Reminding yourself of your objectives;
3. Obtaining a record of events and words exchanged.

Remaining calm comes with practice. It's about keeping your eyes on the bigger picture. Remember that even full-on rows probably won't matter a few weeks from now, and this time next year they will be a distant memory. Don't let yourself become emotionally tangled in the moment. If you need to excuse yourself from the room for a few moments to go to the bathroom, do so. You will win the respect of others by demonstrating that you understand the need to approach conflict from a calm perspective.

Next, remind yourself of your objectives – you have a particular problem that needs solving, and you need to reach some kind of resolution with the minimum of hurt feelings and injury to work relationships. Remind yourself that any work-related argument is much larger than the parties concerned; your primary motive ought to be furthering the aims and success of your organization. Try to shift your focus away from how annoyed or angry you feel with the co-worker in question and instead make sure that you try to secure the best possible outcome for the good of the company. Remind yourself that whilst it's wonderful to be liked by your team, good leadership is not a popularity contest and you are not going to make friends with everyone.

Finally, always get a record of significant conflicts. Following a heated or controversial exchange, write down your version of events and send it via email to all parties involved. Indicate that you felt the debate was worth recording for everyone's sake, and unless they write back to you giving their thoughts to the contrary, you will assume that your account will stand as an accurate reference should any further problems arise. Doing this establishes your reputation as someone who takes disagreements seriously, and it also allows you to cover your own back to some extent should a member of your team later attempt to approach a higher-level manager or launch a formal complaint against you. Although most people will not want to drag out conflict longer than is necessary, there are a few individuals within every large organization who will gladly make trouble wherever possible. It is vital that you understand how important it is to protect yourself from them.

Consider the stakeholders and broader political implications.

Sometimes it is not politically wise to argue, even if you know that you are right. Why? Well, sometimes you need to consider the long-term implications of siding with a particular person, especially if the matter is somewhat trivial, and then use this knowledge to work out how you ought to approach the situation. For example, you may disagree with one of your co-workers, but is your boss or client likely to side with this other party? If this is the case, it may be worth going along with their point of view rather than risk causing unnecessary tensions or rifts.

Bear in mind that compromising can give you leverage later to get you what you want.

Most people think in terms of reciprocation – if you grant them a favor, they often feel beholden to you. In other words, people generally operate on a 'tit for tat' basis. This means that if you choose to compromise with a co-worker, even when you don't have to, they will probably feel as though they 'owe you' a favor later on. Wise leaders use this piece of psychology to their advantage. If you make a point of 'giving in' on relatively minor issues to keep the peace, you can draw upon the store of goodwill you will build up later on when you need something from the person in question. This may sound manipulative, but it is a basic principle of human relationships that most people can and do keep score to some degree. Make sure that you aren't asking for significantly more compromise than you are willing to grant yourself.

Don't just impose your will, unless it's an emergency – people don't easily forgive or forget a tyrant.

If the dispute is ongoing or looks likely to trigger a major rift, schedule a proper meeting to drill down to the real source of the disagreement. Do this as soon as possible. Unless there is a true crisis at work or your team is in urgent need of someone to wade in and restore order, resist the urge to impose your will on people and tell them to obey you purely on the grounds that you are the leader and they are your subordinates.

Such a brutal approach works well in times of emergency and can earn you a grudging respect, but it isn't the best method for long-term engagement and happy working relationships. Make your standard leadership style collaborative and flexible instead of tyrannical, if for no other reason than it gets seriously tiring to be loud and forceful all the time.

WHAT TO DO WITH REALLY ANNOYING CO-WORKERS

You will quickly learn, as a leader, that not everyone you work with is going to like you, respect you, or share your views. We've already looked at how to handle conflict, but what about people who are simply, well, annoying? Here are a few hints on how to handle certain types of personality you may come across in the workplace.

Consider whether their attitude is situation or person-specific.

If you find yourself frequently coming into conflict with a particular person, your first priority should be to ascertain whether it's you they have a problem with, or whether they behave in a similar way to everyone they meet. Notice how they interact with others. You may find that this person has an attitude problem and this discovery may help you to take their behavior less personally.

However, if it's just you they have a problem with, rejoice! Why? Because if you can change your relationship with them, you've solved the problem. Follow the steps in this book and you will make enough of a positive impression on other people that you are likely to earn at least a basic level of respect from this person over time. If not, see it as a lesson in a harsh management reality – that not everyone will grant you the respect you deserve.

If you get the impression that an annoying co-worker or team member is unhappy, make every effort to understand why.

If a member of your team is irritatingly glum or pedantic, schedule a frank discussion about their attitude. Explain it isn't just you it's affecting- it's their own happiness, the other members of their team, and ultimately the performance of the organization as a whole. Rather than treating their problem as an issue within themselves that needs to be fixed, treat their unhappiness as an issue that you can both work jointly to solve. Explain that you know it isn't realistic to expect everyone to enjoy their work and show an outstanding attitude all of the time, but you both have a common interest in enjoying your jobs and adding value to the company. Don't forget to document everything.

Sometimes a single change can stimulate personal growth.

Sometimes people become bored and take it out on others because they are stagnating. Could this be true for that annoying team member? Perhaps they need a change in their routine, some new responsibility, or a new challenge.

Try the broken record technique.

If you are unlucky enough to work with someone who raises the same issues over and over again or who asks you inappropriate questions, use the Broken Record technique. This entails choosing a 'default response' and repeating it every time they trot out the same old question. For example, if you have a team member who continually asks you about the vacation policy, even if it is not your responsibility, try saying something like 'I'm afraid HR is your best bet for that, not me.' Eventually, they will get the message and bother somebody else.

If you have a practical joker in the office, try to channel their efforts elsewhere.

Some people are well-intentioned but nonetheless manage to irritate everyone around them. This is particularly common in 'office jokers,' who seem to make it their mission in life to play pranks or act in a silly fashion as often as possible. To some extent, they should be tolerated – they can add character to a workplace! However, if their antics are having a detrimental effect on the team's productivity, they need to be bought in line. Try a two-pronged approach. Have a one-to-one discussion with them and underline the fact that you appreciate the levity they bring to the workplace, but that they need to tone down their behavior.

At the same time, give them an outlet to channel their energies. Perhaps you could make them responsible for the work socials, for instance. Alternatively, give them some additional work-related challenges that will keep their brains occupied. These sorts of people are often creative and you can make good use of this energy.

If someone thinks they know best all the time, give them a chance to prove it and call their bluff.

If you have to manage a chronic whiner or somebody who subtly suggests that they could do everything better than you if only they were given the opportunity, call their bluff. Make it a point to ask them what they think about difficult issues, and ask them to explain in detail how they would handle a situation. Their responses may be hard to listen to, but they may realize once they are forced to reason a situation aloud, that you are the manager for a reason!

If someone persistently disagrees with your thinking on certain issues but fails to offer constructive suggestions, start asking them for brief written reports containing their input on particular situations. They will soon learn not to casually assert that they could do a better job, or that they have all the answers.

WHEN TO ARGUE AND
WHEN TO LET IT GO

We've already taken a look at how to handle disagreements and how to deal with annoying co-workers, but sometimes you need to ask yourself whether an issue is really worth bothering with in the first place. If you find yourself frequently drawn into conflicts and disagreements – or having to sort them out between two or more of your team members – it may be time to consider whether you are granting too much time to the wrong kinds of issue. Consider the following points when you sense an argument brewing at work.

Sometimes it's better to let someone make a minor mistake by themselves, as long as they have the ability to clear up the mess!
Is a member of your team insistent that they be allowed to do something a certain way, even though it is plain to other people that they are setting themselves up for a fall? One way to handle such a situation is to grant them the chance to teach themselves a lesson. If possible, tell them that you disagree with how they want to handle the scenario, but that you want to let them learn from their own experiences. Take a deep

breath and let them make their own mistakes. Note that you should never do this if the stakes are high, but that allowing someone to make their own errors can be a valuable teaching tool.

Of course, if it turns out that they were right, don't be too proud to admit that they have done a good job. Be humble!

Don't take the fall for someone else.
Although a good leader protects their team to some extent and accepts ultimate responsibility for their outcomes, there is little sense in risking your own reputation for the sake of keeping the peace and going along with a suggestion you feel to be wrong. If someone else's stubborn nature will cost you personally, state your case and then put your foot down.

Ask yourself whether the issue will cease to matter within a week or month.
If the answer is 'No, it won't matter to anyone,' then it probably isn't worth arguing about. Smooth things over as quickly as possible and move onto more important topics. Your time is a valuable commodity, and it makes no sense to argue about petty issues when you have bigger priorities on which to focus. Model this attitude for your team, and they will learn where to direct their own energies.

Sometimes you have to let other people disagree – from separate rooms.
Sometimes it is appropriate to let two of your team members engage in healthy disagreement. However, if they start calling one another names or dragging up issues from the past, it's time to step in and force a truce. This may require you to send one off to engage in an unrelated work task, or even to ask them to sit in separate rooms for a while. If your office atmosphere is informal and the issue is relatively petty, try to

gently point out that they are silly to argue this particular point. This may be enough to help them realize that their time would be better spent elsewhere.

Try to foresee issues that may cause conflict ahead of time, so you can anticipate how best to diffuse the situation. For instance, if you know that two of your team members are likely to get into a disagreement at a particular meeting, you could have a discreet conversation with them both prior to the event and state that whilst you respect that they have a difference of opinion, you are expecting that they will both agree to act like mature adults and share in their commitment to act in the best interests of the company.

Consider the context.
If you catch yourself feeling especially irritable one day for no apparent reason, stay on your guard so as to make sure you don't get into unnecessary arguments. As a rule, do not argue when you are unusually busy, when you are especially tired, or first thing on a Monday morning - this will set an unpleasant tone for the rest of the week.

HOW TO FINALLY START REMEMBERING NAMES

If you manage a large team, you may be required to learn many names in a relatively short space of time. Many leaders find this hard, so here are a few hints that may help!

Put photos of your team members in a convenient file.
Most organizations keep official photographs on file for all employees. Print out an A4 sheet of these photos, with accompanying names, and keep it close to hand. Spend a couple of minutes per day studying this sheet until you learn who's who.

Use their first name in conversation.
Using someone's first name in a greeting and then a couple of times during a conversation will help consolidate it in your memory as your brain will hear the word used in a real-life context. Don't over-use their name – that sounds odd or creepy – but be sure to include it in every meaningful interaction at least once.

Get to know your team as people.

The greater your appreciation of your team members as people, the more readily you will remember their names because they will seem more real and important to you. Make a point of asking after their children, families or about a particular hobby that seems important to them.

If your personality and that of your organization seem suitable, suggest everyone wear name tags for a few days or introduces them whenever they talk to you.

If you are new to an organization and are faced with the task of learning a lot of names in a short amount of time, take a brazen approach and ask everyone to wear small name tags for your first few days. Alternatively, if this tactic isn't quite in keeping with your personality, politely request that everyone introduces themselves by name for the first fortnight you are in your new role.

HOW TO GIVE
VALUABLE FEEDBACK

As a leader, you will be required to give feedback at regular intervals to all members of your team. This can be rewarding when things are going well, but tough when you need to make suggestions as to how people can improve. Read on for a few hints on giving better, more helpful feedback.

Use the Sandwich Technique.
As mentioned previously, the Sandwich Technique is a way of making critical or negative feedback or news more palatable through the delivery of positive reinforcement just prior and after the main content.

When giving feedback, always begin and end by making a positive statement of some kind. For example, you could praise someone's effort on, and attitude towards, a project even if the outcome was not satisfactory.

Focus on goals as well as past performance.
Whether giving good, neutral or negative feedback, move the discussion towards goals as soon as possible. For those who are performing well, goals give them further direction and

incentive to behave in a productive fashion. For those who are underperforming, goals help prevent feelings of hopelessness and helplessness. Never allow someone to go away from a performance review or progress meeting without a good idea of where they should be going next. A lack of focus and certainty will reduce any employee's motivation and lower their performance.

When you take on a leadership role, you will be instructed to follow a particular feedback framework, if your role entails delivering it on a regular basis. It's a good idea to follow the company's prescribed procedures, but if you detect any weaknesses, don't hesitate to approach someone in charge of feedback at HR and politely raise the issue.

Remember the basic guidelines behind all good goal-setting: remember the acronym SMART:

Specific: Goals should address behaviors and targets that can be pinpointed. For example, 'Improve output by 25% within six weeks' is specific, whereas 'improve output soon' is not specific enough.

Measureable: Goals should result in outcomes that can be objectively measured. For example, 'Be in the office on time 100% of the time within the next two weeks.' This is measurable because time can be objectively measured!

Achievable: Goals should actually be feasible.

Relevant: Goals should relate to broader aims and objectives. There is no point in setting a goal if it will not help someone fulfil their job role appropriately.

Time-bound: Goals should always be placed a time context. Goals can span timeframes from days to years, but it is important that the person striving to achieve it have a deadline or similar with which to work.

Focus on the behaviours, not the person.

If you are facing the unpleasant task of admonishing an employee for poor performance or inappropriate behaviour, keep your conversation focused on what they have actually done (or not done), rather than picking holes in their personality. Although it is hard, try to distinguish the person from the way in which they are acting. For example, if a team member is frequently late, stick to the facts when explaining how they need to change, rather than blasting them for their 'sloppy attitude.' Make it clear that you require them to meet certain standards – to be in the office for 8.30am every day unless they are ill or ask permission beforehand to come in later – or else there will be tangible consequences (e.g. a formal written warning).

Regular feedback is important.

If your company doesn't already have a procedure in place by which regular feedback is delivered to employees, make a priority to have one up and running as soon as possible. This can be as simple as a six-month review with a standardised questionnaire, or something more elaborate such as a '360' feedback system in which the employee, their colleagues, and their manager all provide feedback which is then consolidated into a single interview. Ask your peers with similar responsibilities to your own how they approach feedback with their team members. You can save yourself a lot of hassle, time, trial and error by learning from those who have been with the company for longer and understand its culture.

Roadtest your feedback style.

Ask a trusted colleague or friend to give you an honest assessment of your feedback style. Ask them to pretend that they are under your supervision, and that you are giving them feedback. Show them how you deliver positive, neutral and negative feedback. Ask them to comment on your choice of words, pacing, and body language. Ask them to imagine how they would feel leaving the meeting if they were in the position of someone in your team. You may find that you need to communicate more clearly, or perhaps adopt a more encouraging tone of voice. It can be easy to assume that other people infer from us exactly what we are intending to communicate, but often this isn't the case! Minimize the risk of this happening by role playing first.

CONCLUSION

Thank you for choosing and downloading this book! With your newfound knowledge and practical tips to try, you are well-placed to fully develop your leadership potential. Remember that learning to lead well is a lifelong project. Good luck, and here's to your success.

www.ingramcontent.com/pod-product-compliance
Lightning Source LLC
Chambersburg PA
CBHW070414190526
45169CB00003B/1249